THE GRIZZLY BEAR

Alvin and Virginia Silverstein
and Laura Silverstein Nunn
THE MILLBROOK PRESS BROOKFIELD, CONNECTICUT

The authors would like to thank all the dedicated "bear people"
who so kindly provided huge packets of pamphlets, reprints, and other
information. Special thanks to David Mattson, research wildlife biologist of the
U.S.G.S. Forest and Rangeland Ecosystem Science Center, for his careful
reading of the manuscript and many helpful comments and suggestions.
Thanks also to Tamara Culiner of the Yellowstone Grizzly Foundation,
Brian Peck of the Great Bear Foundation, and Louisa Willcox of Wild Forever,
who patiently answered our many telephone questions and
provided fascinating new insights.

Photographs courtesy of Animals, Animals: cover (© Johnny
Johnson), pp. 10 (© Joe McDonald), 12 (© Joe McDonald),
21 (© Charles Palek), 26 (© Joe McDonald), 56 (© Johnny
Johnson); © Henry H. Holdsworth: pp. 4, 25, 30, 31;
Arizona Historical Foundation: p. 6; Craighead Wildlife-
Wildlands Institute: pp. 8, 42; © George Wuerthner: pp. 14,
48; © Erwin & Peggy Bauer/Bruce Coleman, Inc.: pp. 18,
38; © B. D. Wehrfritz: p. 23; Yellowstone National Park
Photo Archives: p. 33; © Leonard Lee Rue III/Bruce
Coleman, Inc.: p. 28; Haynes Foundation Collection,
Montana Historical Society: p. 44

Library of Congress Cataloging-in-Publication Data
Silverstein, Alvin.
The grizzly bear / Alvin and Virginia Silverstein
and Laura Silverstein Nunn.
p. cm. (Endangered in America)
Includes bibliographical references and index.
Summary: Describes the physical characteristics and behavior of the grizzly
bear, its decline in numbers due to human population growth and activities,
and the efforts being made to maintain its population.
ISBN 0-7613-0265-4 (lib. bdg.)
1. Grizzly bear—Juvenile literature. 2. Endangered species—North America—
Juvenile literature. [1. Grizzly bear. 2. Bears. 3. Endangered species.] I.
Silverstein, Virginia B. II. Nunn, Laura Silverstein. III. Title. IV. Series:
Silverstein, Alvin. Endangered in America.
QL737.C27S54 1998
639.97'9784'097—dc21 97-45026 CIP AC

Published by The Millbrook Press, Inc.
2 Old New Milford Road Brookfield, CT 06804

CONTENTS

Two muddy grizzly bear cubs

AMERICA'S SYMBOL OF WILDERNESS

In 1804 the famous explorers Meriwether Lewis and William Clark began a two-year expedition through America's wilderness. During their travels, Lewis and Clark encountered many grizzlies—the largest, most powerful animals in the wild lands of North America. They usually tried to shoot the bears they saw, provoking many grizzly attacks. The explorers' exciting descriptions of their adventures, detailed in their journal published in 1814, were widely read and helped to shape the settlers' attitudes toward the bears.

THE MISTAKEN ENEMY

Native Americans respected the wild animals that shared their homelands. They called the grizzly bear "the beast that walks like a man," and many tribes believed that the grizzly was humans' closest relative. The European settlers who moved into grizzly habitat in the 1800s had a far different view. They feared the grizzly bear because of its enormous size and ravenous appetite. Reports of grizzly at-

Around 1900, when this photograph was taken, grizzly numbers were declining, but no one had yet given thought to the idea of a world without them.

tacks added to their fear. Contrary to popular opinion, though, grizzly bears are not reckless, man-eating beasts. They generally avoid humans. Grizzly attacks usually occur when the bears feel threatened, are surprised, or are protecting their young.

The settlers cut down trees to clear land for farms, roads, and towns. As people moved into grizzly habitat, some grizzlies killed livestock, while others wandered near people's homes, searching for food. Many people were angry and scared. They believed that these animals were not only a nuisance but also very dangerous. Some people killed grizzlies to protect their homes, their livestock, and themselves. Others hunted the bears for their hides. Still others killed the bears as part of a program of extermination sponsored by the government. Grizzly populations were reduced dramatically: from an estimated 50,000 grizzlies in 1800 to fewer than 1,000 in the lower forty-eight states by the 1950s.

BELATED CONCERN

Scientists had known that the grizzly bear was in serious trouble since the early 1900s. But it was not until 1959 that a team of researchers, headed by the brothers John and Frank Craighead, began the first formal study of grizzly bears at Yellowstone National Park. Their goal was to gather information about grizzly bears so that management programs could be developed. The Craighead study team was able to learn a lot about the grizzly's habits and behavior during its life cycle by using radio-tracking devices to record the bears' movements.

The Craighead brothers and other scientists voiced their concerns to the public about the grizzly's plight. They explained that the grizzly bear is a symbol of wilderness, and it needs to be preserved. In 1975 the grizzly bear finally received federal protection under the Endangered Species Act of 1973. A Grizzly Bear Recovery Plan was developed in 1983 and has since gone through several revisions.

Meanwhile, research is still going on. Scientists are using high-tech genetic testing to try to get more realistic estimates of how many grizzly bears really exist and how they are related to one another. It is hoped that genetic studies may help to guide the recovery program. The new knowledge that is being gained may be

John Craighead took this photograph of his brother and their
team as the five of them used a radiotracking system to locate
individual bears in the backcountry.

an important key to helping the grizzly. There is more than wildlife biology involved, however. The continuing story of efforts to
save the grizzly has been marked by disputes and compromises
among environmentalists, developers, and government agencies.
As Grizzly Bear Recovery Coordinator Christopher Servheen puts
it, "The biology is the easy part. It's the politics that can eat you
alive. Recovery of the grizzly bear is not a biological problem, it's
a social problem."

THE GRIZZLY BEAR

The grizzly bear's name has nothing to do with its sometimes frightening reputation, even though it sounds like "grisly." It actually comes from "grizzled," which means streaked with gray, and refers to the silvery-tipped hairs on the bear's coat. Grizzlies are often nicknamed "silvertips." The grizzly bear is a North American subspecies of the brown bear. In Europe and Asia, the "grizzled" bear is commonly called the brown bear.

THE BEAR FAMILY

The grizzly, along with the other bears of North America, belongs to the family *Ursidae* (named for the Latin word for "bear"). The bear family includes eight species (types) of bears around the world. The scientific name for the brown bears is *Ursus arctos*. Two other bear species live in North America as well—the polar bear (*Ursus maritimus*) and the American black bear (*Ursus americanus*). The remaining species live in Asia, South America, and Europe.

An American black bear at rest

The American black bear is a common species. It is also the smallest bear in North America. Black bears live mostly in wooded areas and are excellent tree climbers.

The polar bear lives in areas surrounding the Arctic Ocean. It is slightly larger than the grizzly bear. Some Eskimos hunt polar bears. They are a source of food; their bones are used for utensils; and their hides are made into clothing.

HORRIBLE BEAR

After reading about grizzlies in the journal published by explorers Lewis and Clark, biologist George Ord gave these "tremendous looking animals" the scientific name *Ursus horribilis* ("horrible bear"). Unfortunately, this name contributed to the grizzly bear's bad reputation.

For years, many scientists believed that the grizzly bear was a separate North American species. After studying blood samples taken from bears and their skeletal structure, however, scientists realized that the brown bears all over the world—European, Asian, and North American—should be grouped into one species. Today, the grizzly bear is considered a subspecies of the brown bear and has the scientific name *Ursus arctos horribilis*. Scientists have named another subspecies *Ursus arctos middendorffi*; these are the brown bears living in coastal areas on Kodiak Island, Alaska, and nearby islands. Brown bears that live along the coast and on the surrounding islands are often called coastal brown bears or Alaskan brown bears. Those that live on or near Kodiak Island are called Kodiak bears.

This grizzly has the classic silver-tipped fur that people described as grizzled, or streaked with grey, thereby giving him his name.

WHAT DOES A GRIZZLY LOOK LIKE?

American black bears are sometimes confused with grizzlies. Black bears are not always black. Their coats may be black, dark brown, or cinnamon-brown. A grizzly's coat may also vary in color: black, brown, blond, or a mixture of these.

The grizzly bear and the American black bear do have some very distinctive differences, however. Unlike the black bear, the grizzly has a concave (curved-in) face, short ears, high-humped shoulders, and long, curved claws, which are better equipped for digging up the ground than for climbing trees.

The grizzly bear is much larger than the black bear. A black bear grows to a height of about 5 feet (152 centimeters) when standing, and it weighs 200 to 300 pounds, sometimes up to 500 (100 pounds = 45 kilograms). A male grizzly bear may be up to 8 feet (244 centimeters) tall when standing and weigh 300 to 600 pounds (sometimes more than 800). A female grizzly bear is smaller, weighing only 200 to 400 pounds. Alaskan brown bears and Kodiak bears are generally much larger than grizzly bears and can weigh as much as 1,500 pounds.

HUNGRY AS A BEAR

Bears are well known for their enormous appetites. Grizzly bears belong to the order Carnivora (meat-eaters), which includes the cat and dog families, raccoons, mustelids (weasels, otters, badgers, and

This bear has found a trail of ants which he is busy licking off the tree trunk.

skunks), pinnipeds (seals, sea lions, and walruses), and a few others. Unlike the other carnivores, however, grizzly bears are not entirely meat-eaters. Bears are omnivorous—they eat both meat (including insects) and plants. In fact, a large part of their diet is made up of vegetation.

Grizzly bears spend most of their time foraging (looking for food). In the summer, grizzlies are generally active in the morning and evening and rest during the day and part of the night. In the fall, they forage both day and night to prepare for winter hibernation.

Grizzlies will eat almost anything and consume large amounts of food—a big bear can eat 26 to 35 pounds (12 to 16 kilograms) of food each day. They look for grasses, flowers, sedges, herbs, tubers, roots, bulbs, leaves, berries, and nuts. They also eat honey, ants, grubs, and other insects. (A research team in Yellowstone observed fifty-one grizzly bears feeding on nothing but army cutworm moths and grass for three months each summer. The insects provide a very high-energy food source.) The meat in a grizzly's diet includes bison, elk, deer, salmon, and small animals such as ground squirrels, gophers, and voles. They also eat domestic livestock and poultry, and the young of any species, even bear cubs. Most of the meat that grizzlies eat is usually from animals that have been recently killed, or carrion (animal carcasses). Grizzlies are also attracted to human food, and bears often visit garbage dumps.

GOOD BEAR SENSE

A grizzly bear relies on all its senses—smell, sight, hearing, taste, and touch. Although each sense is important, grizzlies depend most

A Grizzly Tale

JOHN CAPEN "GRIZZLY" ADAMS was a famous hunter who traveled through the California mountains in the 1850s. He liked to capture and tame wild animals. Adams had many scars from his confrontations with grizzly bears, but he was able to tame at least two of them.

One of the first bears that Grizzly Adams captured was a two-and-a-half-year-old cub, which he named Lady Washington. She was not friendly at first, but after intensive training eventually became a trusted companion. Adams captured another grizzly, named Ben Franklin, when he was a newborn cub.

Adams hand-raised Ben Franklin, who turned out to be a good-natured bear. He and Lady Washington followed Adams in his travels. Both bears carried heavy packs, and sometimes Adams even rode on their backs. They slept beside the campfire with him, teamed up with his dog to hunt, and even fought to defend Adams. During the 1850s, Grizzly Adams exhibited his tame grizzlies, along with other animals, at the Pacific Museum in San Francisco.

on their sense of smell. Grizzlies will often stand tall on their hind legs, stick out their noses, and sniff the air. By smelling the air, grizzlies are able to locate food and even detect approaching danger. Their sense of smell is so good that it is often compared to that of a bloodhound. A grizzly's nose can smell a rotting carcass as many as 10 miles (16 kilometers) away.

Many people believe that grizzlies have poor eyesight. But on the contrary, their vision is actually as good as a human's. Their forward-facing eyes, set close together, provide good depth perception. Although their long-distance vision is not as sharp as a human's, grizzlies can track moving prey hundreds of yards away. The myth that bears have poor eyesight probably started because grizzlies often rely on their acute sense of smell rather than their eyesight when evaluating a situation.

Grizzlies have excellent hearing. They can hear the sounds of people talking a quarter of a mile away. Like a dog or cat, grizzlies can also hear in ultrasonic frequencies such as those of a "silent" dog whistle.

Grizzlies have very sensitive lips. Unlike those of most other carnivores, a bear's lips are completely detached from its gums, making them movable. A bear may identify an object by feeling it with its lips as well as smelling it.

Grizzlies also gather information about the environment by touching strange objects with their big paws. Their paws have very sensitive foot pads. Each foot has five short toes with long claws. Their claws are useful tools for handling objects or for digging. Unlike those of many other bear species, the claws of grizzlies are better equipped for digging up the ground in search of food such as tubers, roots, and rodents, than for climbing.

Many people view bears as fascinating animals. Unlike other members of the carnivore family, bears are able to stand up on their hind legs similar to humans. They also walk with their heel and foot flat on the ground. Grizzlies can actually run very fast for short distances despite their slow-moving appearance. They can run twice as fast as humans and can even outrun a racehorse in short sprints of 35 to 40 miles (56 to 64 kilometers) per hour.

This young cub is running as fast as he can, but he is not yet as agile or as quick as his mother.

Grizzlies are curious animals. Scientists believe that they are capable of thought and can learn complicated tasks quickly. Bears have been known to cleverly hide themselves to watch a human passing by. There have been many instances in which a bear who was being followed by a human changed its path so it would not leave any tracks. Bears have also been seen trying to avoid triggering a bear trap or even deliberately setting it off.

Bears have excellent memories. They can remember the areas where the best food sources are. Researchers have observed cubs that traveled with their mother to an area with good food returning to the same spot on a regular basis even without their mother. Bears have also been known to find their way home from a distance of more than 100 miles (160 kilometers). Some bears even managed to overcome obstacles such as big lakes, just to return to their home range.

A GRIZZLY'S LIFE

Grizzlies spend their lives in their own home ranges, where they live, eat, and raise their young. A grizzly's home range is not a single large area; instead, it consists of many areas where food can be found, connected by travel paths. The home range also includes rest areas and protected places where the bear can take shelter or make its den.

Grizzlies are not territorial and do not normally defend their home ranges from other bears. Often the home ranges of individual bears overlap.

The home ranges of male grizzlies are larger than those of females. Males typically roam through a home range of 200 to 500 square miles (518 to 1,295 square kilometers) or even more, depending on the amount of food available. Female grizzlies typically have a smaller home range of 50 to 300 square miles (130 to 777 square kilometers). The home ranges of several females may overlap with that of a male. Females with cubs have the smallest home ranges, to minimize danger to their cubs.

Grizzlies and black bears often live in the same forests, but they have different lifestyles. Grizzlies live in open areas such as

A comfortable spot for this black bear to wait out the danger below

tundra, alpine meadows, and coastlines; black bears are more comfortable traveling through the forests where they are surrounded by trees. Black bears are likely to climb trees at the first sign of danger. Some biologists believe that living in open spaces is what makes grizzlies more aggressive than black bears because there is no way to escape danger. A grizzly is forced to stand its ground and fight, whereas a black bear can climb a tree to escape.

NOT QUITE SOLITARY

Scientists used to believe that grizzly bears were solitary animals. They now realize that bears do not really live isolated lives. In fact, bears actually spend most of their lives interacting with other bears.

Adult male grizzlies can tolerate other bears, but they are not likely to socialize with them. Adult females and their young, on the other hand, may socialize with other grizzly families. Female grizzlies spend much of their lives in the company of other bears. A female grizzly spends two to three years with her cubs after they are born. Once the young bears leave their mother to live independently, the mother is ready to mate again.

Bears may congregate where food sources are plentiful. Brown bears often come together for the annual salmon run at McNeil Falls, Alaska. Every year from June to August, salmon from the Pacific Ocean swim upstream into the McNeil River to lay their eggs. Sometimes forty to eighty bears gather to feast. In Yellowstone, the annual migrations of army cutworm moths are a summer attraction for grizzlies. Large garbage dumps are also a notable site of bear congregations.

These cubs are two years old and still nursing. They could stay with their mother for up to three years, or until her milk dries up.

When a couple of grizzly families live in the same area where food is plentiful (such as at salmon streams), the females will sometimes travel together. They may share babysitting duties and even, on rare occasions, swap cubs. This happens accidentally. Females usually leave their cubs in an area away from a feeding site to keep them safe from adult males. When a mother goes back to retrieve her cubs, the cubs may be unable to recognize her and go to the wrong mother; as many as several litters may follow a single female. Some females may not accept a strange cub and forcibly chase it away, but some will feed another mother's cubs until she comes back to claim them. If their mother does not return, the cubs stay with their new mother and are treated as members of the family.

BEAR TALK

Bears will usually spread out far enough when they feed so that they do not have to interact with one another. When food sources are limited and there are a large number of bears, as at McNeil Falls, direct contact is inevitable. To avoid conflict, bears will form a kind of social structure. Each bear learns its place and knows which other bears are of higher rank and which are lower.

The social rankings are learned through various forms of communication: sounds, body language, and visible signs and scents that bears leave to mark their presence. Communication cues may also be used during the mating season and when more than one bear travels through the same area.

Bears often communicate their intentions through grunts, growls, and loud roars. Body language is also an effective way of expressing their anger and frustration. By gestures such as an open mouth, raised snout, and flattened ears, a bear will let a less dominant bear (one of lower social rank) know that it better not get too close.

Grizzlies generally try to avoid bloodshed. When one bear challenges another, it will walk up to the other bear and look firmly into its eyes. Sometimes the challenger will bluff by charging the other bear and then stopping short. A bear may try to frighten another bear by making as much noise as possible, hitting the ground with its paws. If the other bear does not want to fight, it will lower its head and sit down or start to walk away. But sometimes neither bear backs down, and a fight occurs.

When grizzlies fight, they may wound each other painfully. They charge at each other, hitting with their powerful forelegs and biting with their powerful teeth. They may also lock jaws and wrestle until one bear gives in. The losing bear will lower its head and back away. Dominant males often have many scars. Males are usu-

A fight between two males often results in wounds
from sharp claws and teeth.

It looks like this grizzly is enjoying having his itchy back scratched by the rough bark of the tree.

ally more dominant than females in a fight, but a female will fight to the death to protect her cubs.

Grizzlies, usually males, may also communicate by scraping or chewing the bark off trees and rubbing against the surface, leaving their scent. Whether this is intended to let other bears know who is in the area or for some other reason isn't yet known. Females may leave their mark during the mating season.

Although tree marking can serve as a means of communication, it is possibly done for other reasons. Grizzlies may mark trees to express boredom; to relieve itching; to release tension; to stretch and relax their muscles; to rub off loose hair when they are shedding their thick winter fur in the spring; or to sharpen or trim their long nails (the way a cat does on a scratching post).

READY FOR MATING

Male grizzlies do not usually socialize with females except during the mating season. The female gives off a distinctive scent that tells the male that she is in estrus, or ready for mating. Often, male grizzlies must compete with other bears to mate with the female. When there is a small population of grizzlies, the mating pair will stay together for two to three weeks. However, in a larger population both the male and female may wander off and may have several different mating partners. Once the courtship ends, the male and female go their separate ways, and the female is left to raise the cubs by herself.

When a male and female grizzly mate, sex cells (sperm) from the male combine with sex cells (ova or eggs) from the female in a process called fertilization. A fertilized egg contains hereditary information from both the father and the mother and is the start of a new life. But in grizzlies that new life does not begin developing right away. The grizzly's fertilized eggs do not immediately settle down to grow inside the female's uterus. Scientists call this process *delayed implantation*, and there is an important reason for the delay. The grizzly female spends the summer and fall gorging on food and storing it in the form of fat. Both she and her new cubs will get nourishment from her body fat during the winter. If she does not have enough fat reserves to enable her to meet the additional needs of pregnancy through the period of hibernation (deep sleep), the partially developed eggs will not implant and will then be reabsorbed by her body.

When the grizzly cubs are born, in January or February, their mother is asleep! Several months before, she had settled into a cozy den and had begun to hibernate. The female may give birth to one to four bear cubs, although two is most typical. Each cub is born blind, hairless, and almost totally helpless. It weighs only a pound

Grizzly cubs, just a few days old

or less—the size of a chipmunk. It is hard to believe that the cub may grow to 800 pounds (360 kilograms). The mother wakes briefly to lick her newborn cubs clean, then goes back to sleep for a few months. The cubs snuggle against her, drink milk from the nipples on her belly, doze, and grow.

SURVIVING IN THE WILD

In the springtime, the mother grizzly and her cubs are ready to leave their winter den. The bear cubs have now grown to about 7 pounds (3 kilograms) and are strong enough to get out into the real world. During the winter months, the cubs spent the time bonding with their mother even though she was sleeping. Their mother was their source of food and warmth.

Now the mother serves as a teacher and disciplinarian. By watching her, the bear cubs learn how to survive in the wild: what foods to eat, where and how to get them, where to den, and, especially, to be aware of dangers, such as wolves, humans, and adult male grizzlies.

A mother grizzly will fight fiercely to defend her cubs. At the first sign of danger she will chase them away until it is safe. If any cubs disobey her, she will discipline them with a growl, bite, or swat. But the mother grizzly must spend a lot of time getting food to satisfy her own needs and make milk for the cubs. She cannot always be around to protect her cubs, and they cannot defend themselves yet. So some fall prey to predators. As many as half of all cubs do not make it to breeding age.

These cubs are about three or four months old, and stay close to their mother when she becomes alert and wary.

These young cubs have been rolling together in the gravel. If they are the firstborn of a young mother, there is a chance that she is not keeping an eye on them. Older mothers who have had many litters tend to be more careful with their cubs.

Grizzly cubs spend time playing with each other. They sniff and poke and swat each other and roll about in rough-and-tumble wrestling. Play helps the cubs to sharpen their reflexes, senses, and coordination.

Grizzly cubs usually stay with their mother for two to three years. They may continue to nurse during this time until their mother's milk starts to dry up. This is a sign that she is ready to mate again. The mother will stop taking care of her cubs and chase them away when they try to get near. If the mother finds another mate and the cubs are still around, they will quickly run away and live on their own. The young bears may stay together for another year or longer, until they themselves are ready to mate. Grizzlies become sexually mature between four and six years of age, although some are not ready until later.

A WINTER SLUMBER

During the summer and autumn months, bears have insatiable appetites. They are constantly hungry because they have to bulk up for winter hibernation. Bears may spend twenty out of twenty-four hours eating and gain as much as 40 pounds (18 kilograms) each week. They have been known to consume as much as 20,000 calories each day, which would be like a person eating forty hamburgers and forty ice-cream sundaes in a twenty-four-hour period!

In October or November, the bears become rather sluggish. They stop eating and look for a den for the winter. Grizzlies dig their own dens with their claws, usually on a mountain slope where the winter snow will serve as insulation. Grizzlies often dig under the roots of a tree or may den in a rock cave.

Winter hibernation is essential for a bear's survival. It is able to survive cold weather and a limited food supply by sleeping. Hibernation is not ordinary sleep but rather an energy-saving process that allows bears to go through long periods without eating and still maintain their body weight. They are able to survive and feed off their body fat throughout the winter and into spring.

Bears' hibernation is quite different from that of other mammals, such as squirrels and chipmunks. The body temperature of a

This bear den is
in Yellowstone
National Park.

hibernating squirrel may drop to almost freezing, which does not allow it to awaken easily. A hibernating bear's body temperature, on the other hand, only drops 5 to 9 degrees Fahrenheit (3 to 7 degrees Celsius) from its normal range of 87.8 to 99 degrees Fahrenheit (31 to 37.4 degrees Celsius). This means that bears can wake up almost instantly if danger approaches.

There are significant changes in the bear's body systems during hibernation, however. Its heartbeat slows from 40 to 50 beats per minute down to 8 to 10 beats per minute. Its breathing also slows down, so that it uses only half the oxygen it does when it is active. The chemical reactions that go on in the bear's body (its metabolism) are also greatly slowed, reducing its need for food. (Its stored fat would not be enough to last the winter if it were active.) The

Some Restless Sleepers

ALTHOUGH BEARS *can* sleep straight through the winter into spring, grizzlies occasionally can be seen wandering around in the middle of the winter. At Yellowstone, since wolves have been reintroduced, wildlife biologists are finding that the bears are waking up more often, to take advantage of the leftovers from the wolf kills. In Canada, where both bears and wolves are more plentiful, this is a common occurrence.

bear's kidneys and digestive tract have shut down completely. Unlike other mammals, bears do not eat, drink, urinate, or defecate during hibernation. Scientists are not sure how the process works, but they believe that the urine gets reabsorbed in the bear's body.

The bears leave their winter den in March, April, or May, depending on weather conditions, their health, and their remaining fat reserves. Adult males usually leave their dens first. Females with cubs are the last to leave their winter dens. Bears lose a great deal of weight during hibernation. Adult males and adolescent bears lose between 15 and 30 percent of their weight. A female with newborn cubs may lose as much as 40 percent of her weight.

Bears emerging from hibernation are very sluggish for several weeks until their metabolic system returns to normal. Until then, they are not very hungry. When their appetite finally comes back, they feed on carrion, such as elk or deer that did not survive the winter, as well as emerging green vegetation.

ON THE BRINK OF EXTINCTION

Today's population of about 1,000 grizzlies in the lower forty-eight states (excluding Alaska and Hawaii) occupies less than 2 percent of their original range.

Grizzlies live in five ecosystems in these states: Yellowstone (northwest Wyoming, south-central Montana, and eastern Idaho), Northern Continental Divide (northwest Montana and northern Idaho), Cabinet-Yaak (northwest Montana), and Selkirk (northern Idaho).

The last known wild grizzly was seen in the Selway-Bitterroot ecosystem (central Idaho) in the 1940s, but recovery efforts are under way. At present, there are no grizzlies in another former home ecosystem, the San Juan Mountains (Colorado).

In western Canada and Alaska, which were not as heavily settled, the decline has not been as steep. An estimated 41,000 grizzly bears still remain in these areas: about 10,000 in British Columbia, another 2,000 to 3,000 in other Canadian provinces, and the rest in Alaska.

WHY THE GRIZZLY DECLINED

Excessive extermination campaigns, hunting, and habitat loss have been the main reasons for the grizzly's decline. Human settlement in grizzly habitat had made interaction between humans and bears more likely. Sometimes a grizzly would attack a human if it was frightened or threatened. Although grizzly attacks are extremely rare, some people began to view the grizzly bear as "a filthy, murderous animal." They quickly targeted them as pests that had to be removed.

In Canada and some parts of Alaska, it is legal to hunt grizzly bears. Each year, wildlife managers decide how many bears can be killed without threatening their population. In the fall, if that number has not been reached, a hunting season is declared. Hunting continues until the year's quota of bear kills is reached. Sometimes the bear-hunting season is considerably shortened or even canceled when the quota is met because of other causes of death.

Some grizzlies are killed because hunters have mistaken them for black bears during the black-bear hunting season. Young grizzlies have the greatest mortality—as much as 40 percent die during their first year of life. Some bear cubs may be killed by predators such as wolves, mountain lions, and adult grizzlies. Other bears may die of starvation and disease.

Poachers (people who hunt animals illegally) kill grizzlies every year. The body parts of bears are often sold to Asian countries, where some people believe that certain bear parts have magical powers or can cure diseases. Bear body parts are highly profitable on the black market: A single bear claw can sell for up to $250; a whole bear hide in good condition can bring up to $2,000; and a bear's gallbladder can sell for up to $5,000.

The slow reproduction rate of grizzlies makes it difficult for them to thrive. A female is not sexually mature until she is about five years old. She then mates every three or more years. When a large number of grizzlies are killed in a single year, it is very hard for them to rebuild their families.

Wildlife biologists are also concerned about inbreeding among grizzly bears. As the grizzly population continues to decline, some bears are forced to mate with family members. Inbreeding can lead to a loss of genetic diversity within the grizzly population. Inbred bears may be more susceptible to disease and may have difficulties in reproducing.

Because grizzly bears have such tremendous appetites, the lack of food sources has had a strong impact. However, the loss of natural plant and animal food due to development from human activities is an insignificant threat compared with the presence of people with guns.

NEW THREATS

Grizzlies in the Greater Yellowstone ecosystem have had one of their favorite foods threatened: spawning cutthroat trout, which is a rich source of protein and fat and is easily digested. In 1994 a number of people reported catching lake trout in Yellowstone Lake, where cutthroat normally swim. Lake trout are not native to these waters and do not move naturally into the lake from other waters

This cub, five months old, is trying to figure out how to break open this pinecone.

in the park. Researchers believe that the lake trout were brought to the lake illegally. Lake trout prey on cutthroat trout, and therefore are a threat to them as well as to grizzlies and other species that depend on cutthroat trout as a food source. In 1995 tens of thousands of lake trout inhabited the Yellowstone Lake.

Whitebark pinecones are another important part of the grizzly's diet; they are high in calories, and grizzlies load up on them for hibernation. They are also foods that sustain army cutworm moths, which are another food source for the bears. Now, however, whitebark pines are threatened. An exotic fungus called blister rust is infecting almost 90 percent of the whitebark pine trees in Glacier National Park (northern Montana in the Northern Divide ecosystem), and parts of the Greater Yellowstone ecosystem. The pines are also threatened by global climate warming.

SAVING THE GRIZZLY

By the start of the twentieth century, grizzly populations were dwindling at an alarming rate. In the early 1800s, there were an estimated 10,000 grizzlies in California alone. But by 1922, the last California grizzly was killed. Ironically, the grizzly bear is California's state animal, and the grizzly is pictured on its state flag.

STUDYING GRIZZLIES IN HOPES OF THEIR SURVIVAL

Scientists realized that one way to try to save the grizzly was to learn more about them. In 1944, biologists Adolf and Olaus Murie tried to study grizzly bears at Yellowstone National Park. The Muries were able to observe grizzlies only from a distance, often while the bears were feeding at garbage dumps. In 1952, scientist Albert W. Erickson developed a method that would make it possible to study a grizzly up close. Erickson and his study team would trap a bear by its foot and tranquilize it by throwing an ether mask over its face. Erickson struggled with more than a hundred grizzlies during this process. Some of the bears were killed or injured, and members of the study team suffered some injuries as well.

By the late 1950s, more advanced techniques were developed for capturing grizzlies. Scientists used special guns with darts filled with anesthetics that could safely tranquilize an animal so it could be tagged and marked for identification.

THE CRAIGHEAD STUDY

Wildlife scientists Frank and John Craighead, identical twin brothers, had done major studies on wild animals such as hawks, owls, elk, and coyotes. When they found out that the grizzly bear was in trouble, they became intrigued and decided to make it their next study project.

In 1957, the Craigheads started to write a proposal about the grizzly bear. They wanted to gather information about the grizzlies at Yellowstone National Park: the size of their population; their feeding, reproduction, and other behavior; and the reasons for their deaths. The Craighead brothers hoped that the information they uncovered would be used to help manage and protect grizzly bears so they could continue to survive in the wild.

In 1959, Frank and John Craighead arrived at Yellowstone National Park to begin the first formal study of grizzly bears. They used different types of bear traps to capture bears. A steel trap, called the culvert trap, was baited with some of the bears' favorite foods, such as honey, fruit juice, or beef. Once a bear was inside, it triggered the door, which then closed after it. The bear was then shot with a tranquilizer gun.

The foot snare, typically used in the woods, was another effective bear trap. When the trap was triggered, a noose tightened around the bear's leg, and the bear was unable to escape. It was then tranquilized with a dart gun.

The researchers had to learn how to estimate the bear's weight before administering the drug. The proper dosage depended on its weight. Too much of the drug could make the bear sick or even kill it. If the dosage was not enough, the bear could wake up too soon and endanger the lives of the researchers. A spare tranquilizing needle was kept on hand just in case.

Once the grizzly was tranquilized, the researchers put numbered metal tags on both of the bear's ears. They also attached streamers patterned with different colors to its ears so they could identify the bear from a distance. Using permanent ink, the bear was also marked with a number under its leg. The researchers then measured the bear's weight, height, and the size of its feet. They also took a mold of its teeth with a special kit to estimate the bear's age. (A bear's tooth is like a tree trunk—it grows a new ring every year.) Blood samples were also taken so that scientists could learn how a bear's body systems work.

RADIO BEAR

The Craighead brothers wanted to use radiotelemetry for their study. By tracking a grizzly's movements with a radio-tracking device, they could learn more about its behavior. In 1961, Joel Varney and Richard Davies from the Philco Corporation, a manufacturer of radios and televisions, were asked to develop a radio-tracking de-

The Craighead brothers examine a tranquilized large male grizzly. The radio collar weighed about two pounds but did not appear to bother any of the grizzlies who wore them.

vice, consisting of a sturdy collar containing batteries, a transmitter, and an antenna. The radio device would make beeps that the scientists could pick up with an electronic receiver from miles away. The louder the beeps, the closer the bear; when the beeps got louder and softer, the bear was moving around; when the beeps were constant, the bear was resting or sleeping.

In September 1961, Davies developed the first radio collar for bears and tested it on Bear Number 40, who became the world's first "radio bear." She was a good candidate because she was fairly shy and not aggressive. To honor Davies, the scientists later named the bear Marian, after Davies's wife. Other bears that were collared were also given nicknames. Over the years, Varney and Davies made lighter and more effective radio devices.

GRIZZLY POLITICS

In August 1967, two women were attacked and killed by grizzlies on the same night, in two different places in Glacier National Park in Montana. These incidents terrified the public. The National Park Service decided changes needed to be made in bear-management policies. The new policy aimed to maintain wildlife in as close to a natural state as possible.

By late 1967, Yellowstone had a new superintendent and a head biologist. They introduced strict fishing regulations, stopped the annual hunts to reduce elk herds, and developed a more natural fire policy. These changes were important for the Yellowstone grizzlies, but another change in policy had a far more dramatic effect.

For more than eighty years, ever since 1872 when Yellowstone was created as our first national park, grizzlies in the area had been feeding at numerous open garbage dumps in and around the park. The park management had encouraged this practice: The bears were helping to get rid of refuse, and park visitors were able to observe them safely when they came to the dumps to feed. The garbage dumps were a rich and dependable source of high-energy food. However, the new park officials decided to close the garbage dumps so that the grizzlies could return to a more natural state. The

Bear shows were well-organized and well-attended even up to the early 1940s when this picture was taken. Food waste from a nearby hotel was regularly dumped on concrete platforms and the grizzlies soon became dependent on this source of food.

Craigheads felt that closing the garbage dumps abruptly would be disastrous, forcing hungry grizzlies into campgrounds, where they would learn to associate food with people and dangerous conflicts would result. They warned that the Yellowstone grizzlies might become extinct within twenty years unless the park officials changed their methods of bear management.

At first it seemed that the Craigheads' fears had become a reality. As the dumps were closed, from 1968 through 1971, many grizzlies had a hard time adjusting. There was a dramatic increase in grizzly visits to campgrounds. The response of the Park Service was a "control action," in which some grizzlies were trapped and moved out of the park area and "problem bears" were killed. As a direct result of abruptly closing the dumps, more than 120 bears were killed during a three-year period. Meanwhile, other grizzlies moved into the surrounding national forests in search of food and were killed during legal sport-hunting seasons.

The dispute between the Craigheads and the park management heated up, and the Park Service began to place restrictions on the biologists' studies. The Craigheads' contract expired in 1970, and they were offered a new one stipulating that they would not say or write anything about grizzlies without the approval of the federal government. The Craigheads refused to sign the new contract and left Yellowstone in 1971.

COULD THE GRIZZLIES RETURN TO WILD WAYS?

The National Park Service's treatment of the Craigheads and their study sparked a furious public debate. Some scientists and citizens pointed to the increased deaths of Yellowstone grizzlies and said that their population had already reached a dangerously low level. They wondered whether, after generations of easy living at the garbage dumps, the grizzlies could relearn how to live on natural foods—and even if they did, were there enough natural foods left to support them? In response to public pressure, the Interagency Grizzly Bear Study Team (IGBST) was created in 1974 to study and evaluate the grizzly population at Yellowstone. A report issued in 1975 praised the Craigheads' research and criticized the Park Service's efforts, stating that its estimates of the bear populations between 1971 and 1973 had no scientific basis and its grizzly management policies were inadequate. It seemed that the Yellowstone grizzly population had been pushed to the brink of extinction.

In 1975, the grizzly bear finally received legal protection and was listed as a threatened species under the Endangered Species Act. (The ESA defines a threatened species as one that is likely to become endangered in the near future in all or most of its range.) At Yellowstone, measures were taken to help the grizzly population, then estimated at about 200 bears, to survive. In an important step, all sport hunting of grizzly bears was stopped in the three states surrounding Yellowstone. The Endangered Species Act also provided a higher level of protection for the grizzlies throughout the area.

In the years that followed, the Yellowstone grizzlies proved to be more adaptable than many scientists had expected. They learned again to hunt and fish and took advantage of the growth in elk and bison herds and cutthroat trout populations that were occurring as a result of the new conservation policies in the park. This promising trend was helped by the creation, in 1983, of the Interagency Grizzly Bear Committee (IGBC), composed of members of federal and state management agencies from Montana, Wyoming, and Idaho. It was agreed that the efforts toward recovery of the Yellowstone grizzly bear population would emphasize management of the whole ecosystem.

LEGAL BATTLES

In 1982, the U.S. Fish and Wildlife Service (FWS) submitted the first draft of the Grizzly Bear Recovery Plan. One of the goals of the plan was to recover grizzly populations in all of the ecosystems known to have a suitable habitat. A goal for overall recovery was set: If the total number of grizzlies in the lower forty-eight states, spread over perhaps half a dozen ecosystems, could be brought up to 1,500, the species could be considered successfully recovered. It would be able to survive on its own, without further government help. Thus the grizzly bear could be "delisted"—removed from the list of threatened species given protection under the Endangered Species Act. This is the ultimate goal for all the recovery programs for threatened and endangered species. Some wildlife biologists and conservationists, however, have expressed concern about what might happen if the grizzly were delisted too soon, before the species had truly reached the point where it could thrive on its own.

RESTORING MISSING LINKS

The first draft of the FWS Grizzly Bear Recovery Plan called for evaluating the Bitterroot ecosystem, in central Idaho and western Montana, as a potential recovery area. An evaluation study, conducted from 1985 to 1990, found no existing grizzly bear population but considered the habitat to be suitable. According to the

The Selway River by Bad Luck Creek in the Bitterroot Wilderness, Idaho

proposal, four to six grizzlies per year would be moved into Bitter-root over a period of five years. The bears would be taken from British Columbia and start a population that would grow to a target of about 280 bears within forty to sixty years. The Bitterroot recovery plan was approved by the IGBC in 1994, and the FWS began an environmental impact study. A similar plan was developed for the North Cascades ecosystem, in Washington.

Wildlife scientists and members of conservationist organizations such as Defenders of Wildlife have found a lot to like in the recovery plan. The Bitterroot site may be especially important in helping to ensure the grizzly's long-term survival. Not only will it provide an additional population of bears, increasing the current total by nearly a third, but it has a strategic location. Its northeast tip is 45 miles (72 kilometers) from the Northern Continental Divide ecosystem, its northwest end only 37 miles (60 kilometers) from the Cabinet-Yaak ecosystem, and its southern end is 240 miles (386 kilometers) from Yellowstone. If a thriving grizzly population is reestablished in Bitterroot, bears wandering from its edges might mingle with grizzlies from populations in the other ecosystems. Bitterroot could thus serve as a key link in helping to prevent inbreeding.

The proposed plan has also gained support from the Idaho timber industry and other groups that have traditionally opposed environmentalists on issues concerning endangered species. In a give-and-take compromise among the various groups—not only conservationists and wildlife specialists but also loggers, ranchers, oil companies, and various other interests—the Citizen Management Committee Alternative (also known as the ROOTS Alternative, named for a timber industry organization) was drawn up. Grizzlies would be introduced only into the Selway Bitterroot Wilderness (2,168 square miles, or 5,615 square kilometers) and could expand into a larger recovery area, to be determined by a Citizen Management Committee chosen from a list of candidates supplied by the governors of Idaho and Montana. The committee would have the power to make key management decisions, and the reintroduced bears would be classified as "experimental, nonessential." This would allow the bears in the recovery area to be removed or killed if they came in conflict with human activities.

By 1997, though, the Bitterroot proposal was still bogged down in controversy. Alternative plans were still being considered. In addition, the National Marine Fisheries Service called for studies of the impact on salmon and steelhead fishing, which would delay the completion of the environmental impact studies. The state governors and legislatures were still opposing even the ROOTS Alternative, despite the fact that a poll in Idaho showed that 62 percent of the local citizens supported grizzly reintroduction. Amid talk of eliminating Bitterroot from the recovery plan, Secretary of the Interior Bruce Babbitt announced that the federal government would not back down. Yet there was some question of where bears could be obtained if reintroduction plans went ahead. Canadians have become increasingly concerned about the prospects of their own grizzly populations. Some of them oppose the idea of having Canadian bears sent to new homes below the border. How this controversy will be resolved is one of the many questions remaining in the story of grizzlies in America.

THE GRIZZLY'S FUTURE

In the early 1980s, Dr. Stephen French, an emergency-room physician in Evanston, Wyoming, treated several patients who had been injured by grizzly bears in nearby Yellowstone. He became curious about the bears and began to read about them. Soon he and his wife, Marilynn Gibbs-French, realized that there were still many questions about grizzly behavior—especially about how the grizzlies had been living since the garbage dumps in the park were closed. In 1983 the Frenches began a field study of the Yellowstone grizzlies. They formed the Yellowstone Grizzly Foundation (YGF), an independent research and educational organization, to coordinate their efforts. The Frenches wanted to observe the bears' natural behavior—how they interact with their environment, not with the human researchers. They used spotting scopes and telephoto lenses to observe the bears from a distance.

Over the years the Frenches and other researchers working with them have made thousands of observations, described in detailed field notes and film records. They have watched as grizzlies returned to natural food sources, stalking and killing elk calves, fishing for cutthroat trout in the shallow streams where they spawn, and raking up loose rocks on the mountain slopes to feed on migrating army cutworm moths while they rest during the summer days. YGF researchers have found that individual grizzlies eat hundreds of thousands of moths each year and are now trying to determine whether there are any harmful effects from pesticide residues that may have built up in the moths' bodies when they were feeding on farmlands before their migration to Yellowstone. The Frenches, working with state and federal agencies, have developed techniques for genetic studies that can help to establish exactly how many bears are now living in the Greater Yellowstone ecosystem and whether—after the many deaths—their population still has enough genetic diversity to thrive.

GRIZZLY GENETICS

When Lance Craighead was a teenager, his father, Frank, and uncle, John Craighead, were in the midst of their classic study of the Yellowstone grizzlies. Lance and his cousin Johnny even went along on some of the field trips. So it is not too surprising that Lance Craighead chose a project involving grizzly bears for his Ph.D. studies. For seventeen years, in the foothills of the Western Brooks Range in Alaska, Harry Reynolds of the Alaska Fish and Game Department had studied the local grizzly population. A total of 256 individual bears were captured during the study. Blood samples were collected from the bears, along with small plugs of ear tissue obtained while attaching ear tags. Using samples collected by Harry Reynolds, and working with researchers in university genetics laboratories, Lance Craighead and his study team carefully isolated DNA, the chemical of heredity, from each sample.

By comparing distinctive parts of the DNA that may differ from one bear to another, the researchers were able to identify the relationships among many of the bears they had studied. They found, for example, that it is common for a female bear to breed with more than one male, so that some of her cubs may have different fathers. Craighead believes that this competition among males during the breeding season helps to maintain genetic diversity among the grizzly bear population.

The Alaskan grizzlies are part of a large population connected to other large grizzly groups. The findings for these bears thus provide a measure of the genetic diversity in wild grizzly populations, to which more isolated populations such as the Yellowstone grizzlies can be compared.

At Yellowstone, the Frenches are trying to develop methods for studying grizzly genetics without actually capturing the bears and taking specimens. They have found that the roots of the hairs that grizzlies rub off on trees and other objects contain enough DNA for genetic testing. By comparing the DNA of today's Yellowstone grizzlies to samples taken from pelts, bones, and teeth of grizzlies that lived there in the past, scientists will be able to trace the changes in the population over the years and determine how much genetic diversity has been lost. "DNA fingerprinting" can also be used to identify individual bears.

RESTORING HABITAT

The new emphasis on habitat security as a key to grizzly recovery is resulting in some encouraging progress. In Glacier National Park,

Superhighway for Animals

ENVIRONMENTALISTS HAVE proposed a bold (and controversial) new plan to help the survival of the grizzly bear and other endangered species: building an 1,800-mile (2,897-kilometer) animal-friendly corridor extending from Yellowstone to the Yukon in Canada. This project, known as "Y2Y," would involve replanting forests, limiting cattle grazing, and constructing protected overpasses over highways. Linking the isolated Yellowstone grizzly population with the grizzlies in Canada would allow an exchange of genes that would keep the Yellowstone bears from getting too inbred. For now, Y2Y is just a dream. Making it a reality would require an enormous amount of money, ingenuity in overcoming practical problems (how do you get a bear to use an overpass?), and a massive campaign to persuade the people in the nearby areas to accept animal traffic in their midst.

in the Northern Divide ecosystem, some roads are being closed each year. The roads are bulldozed and seeded or planted with trees so that they can return to a wild state. Many miles of roads will eventually be closed, greatly expanding the amount of undisturbed habitat for grizzlies. (The bears normally avoid an area within three-tenths to a half mile of active roadways.) Making the area less accessible to poachers will also help to protect the grizzlies there. Similar efforts are under way in the Gallatin National Forest in the Yellowstone ecosystem, where the Forest Service has already closed about 100 miles (160 kilometers) of roads on the border with Yellowstone National Park.

Many problems still remain, however. Oil and gas development and timber cutting, allowed in federal lands in the Greater Yellowstone area, may affect some grizzly habitat. (Clearcut logging eliminates the forest cover where grizzlies and other species like to hide.) Grizzly habitat is also being broken up by development of private land around the national forests. Even when they are not developed, the private lands used by grizzlies as sources of natural foods or as travel routes can be dangerous places for the bears. Biologist Marilynn Gibbs-French notes that although private lands represent only about 1 percent of the Yellowstone ecosystem, they account for up to two-thirds of all the conflicts between grizzlies and humans in the ecosystem.

Despite the threats still hanging over the grizzly's future, bear watchers in the Yellowstone area have been noticing some encouraging signs. In 1996, grizzlies were spotted "everywhere"—including parts of the ecosystem where they had not been seen for forty or fifty years. The YGF team noted that more cubs than usual were born—more than seventy—and the number of new births was greater than the number of deaths.

WHY SAVE THE GRIZZLIES?

Preserving the threatened populations of grizzly bears in the lower forty-eight states will take a continuing effort, involving money, labor, and goodwill. Is it worth it to save a predator with a bad reputation?

Marilynn Gibbs-French notes that there is still important knowledge to be gained from the grizzly. A better understanding of the grizzly's unusual adaptations to hibernation, for example, may provide insights into some human ailments such as kidney failure, heart disease, osteoporosis, and eating disorders. The amazing ability of the bears to maintain their bone and muscle mass even though they are inactive for months may hold the key to allowing astronauts to go on long zero-gravity space voyages.

Purely practical considerations, however, are not the most important reason to save the grizzly. This huge mammal is a key part of a complex ecology. By preserving its habitat in order to allow it to survive, we will also preserve the hundreds of other animal and plant species that make up the wilderness communities—a heritage we can save for future generations. As Frank Craighead has written, "Alive, the grizzly is a symbol of freedom and understanding—a sign that man can learn to conserve what is left of the Earth. Extinct, it will be another fading testimony to things man should have learned more about but was too preoccupied with himself to notice."

FINGERTIP FACTS

Height (length)   An adult grizzly's height can range from 5 to 8 feet (152 to 244 centimeters) tall when standing. Females are typically smaller than males.

Weight   Adult male grizzlies weigh about 300 to 600 pounds (sometimes more than 800). Females weigh between 200 and 400 pounds (100 pounds = 45 kilograms).

Color   The grizzly's coat may be black, cinnamon, red, blond, or a mixture of these colors. But the grizzly is known for its typical silvery-tipped hairs, or "grizzled" look.

Food   Grizzlies eat grasses, flowers, herbs, tubers, roots, bulbs, leaves, fruits, and seeds. They also eat honey, ants, grubs, and other insects. Plants and insects make up most of their diet. To a lesser extent grizzlies eat meat, including fish, moose, elk, deer, small animals (ground squirrels, rodents, etc.), domestic livestock and poultry, and the young of any species, even bear cubs. Grizzlies will also feed on animals that have been recently killed or on carrion (animal carcasses).

Reproduction	Grizzlies are ready to breed between four and six years of age. Females give birth during winter hibernation; litters average two cubs, but there may be as many as four. Females breed every three or more years.
Care for young	The female takes full responsibility for her cubs; she nurses them and feeds them; she also teaches them where to find food and take shelter. The male's responsibility ends after fertilizing the female.
Range	There are scattered populations in Wyoming, Montana, Idaho, and Washington. More significant numbers are found in Canada and Alaska.
Population size	About 1,000 grizzlies remain in the lower 48 states; about 50,000 in Canada and Alaska.
Social behavior	Grizzlies are solitary animals except during the mating season and salmon runs. Females are more sociable than males; they raise their families and may travel with other mothers. Young grizzlies may also travel, eat, and play together.
Life span	Grizzlies live about 15 to 20 years in the wild; 30 or more years in captivity.

FURTHER READING

Books:

Calabro, Marian. *Operation Grizzly Bear*. New York: Four Winds Press, 1979.

Craighead, Frank C., Jr. *Track of the Grizzly*. San Francisco: Sierra Club Books, 1979.

Craighead, John J., Sumner, Jay S., and Mitchell, John A. *The Grizzly Bears of Yellowstone: Their Ecology in the Yellowstone Ecosystem, 1959-1992*. Washington: Island Press, 1995.

McNamee, Thomas. *The Grizzly Bear*. New York: Lyons and Burford, 1997.

Patent, Dorothy Hinshaw. *Bears of the World*. New York: Holiday House, 1980.

Patent, Dorothy Hinshaw. *The Way of the Grizzly*. New York: Clarion Books, 1987.

Schullery, Paul. *The Bears of Yellowstone*. Worland, WY: High Plains Publishing Company, 1992.

Stone, Lynn M. *Grizzlies*. Minneapolis: Carolrhoda Books, Inc., 1993.

Pamphlets and Reports:

Gunther, Kerry, and Biel, Mark, *Bear Information Book 1996*, Yellowstone National Park.

Norton, Matt, *Report: Grizzly Bear Recovery Impacts on Recreation Within Grizzly Bear Recovery Zones*, Greater Ecosystem Alliance, July 1994.

Shaffer, Mark L., *Keeping the Grizzly Bear in the American West*, The Wilderness Society, December 1992.

U.S. Fish and Wildlife Service, *Grizzly Bear Information Sheet*, August 1995.

U.S. Fish and Wildlife Service, *Grizzly Bear Recovery Plan*, 1993.

Internet Resources:

http://www.avicom.net/ceri/ (Craighead Environmental Research Institute—links to grizzly genetics and distribution)

http://www.defenders.org/grizza.html (Grizzly bear facts and photos)

http://www.defenders.org:80/bitter.html (The Return of the Grizzly—Bitterroot recovery plan)

http://www.desktop.org:80/ygff/YGF.GrizInfo.html (Grizzly bear information and links to research articles)

http://www.ilhawaii.net/~stony/lore48.html (Mt. Shasta grizzly legend)

http://www.nature.net.com/bears/brown.html (The Bear Den—information on brown and grizzly bears)

http://www.netway.net:80/cwc/F94/F94-2.html (Black Bear or Grizzly Bear?—comparison and quiz)

http://www.wwfcanada.org/facts/grizzly.html (Grizzly bear fact sheets)

http://www.yellowstonepark.com/this_issue/grizzlies.html (Yellowstone Journal Online)

FOR MORE INFORMATION

Craighead Wildlife-Wildlands Institute
5200 Upper Miller Creek Road
Missoula, MT 59803
(406) 251-3867

Great Bear Foundation
P.O. Box 1289
Bozeman, MT 59771
(800) 822-6525

U.S. Fish & Wildlife Service
Grizzly Bear Recovery Coordinator
Forestry Sciences Laboratory
University of Montana
Missoula, MT 59812

Yellowstone Grizzly Foundation
581 Expedition Drive
Evanston, WY 82930
(307) 734-8643

INDEX